How to Be a Cool Kid

Middle Schoolers Guide to Being Cool
and Staying Out of Trouble

SUNRISE TO SUNSET
PUBLISHING

TABLE OF CONTENTS

INTRODUCTION

L ife goes by quick. One minute you're anxious to grow up, the next you're stressed at how many responsibilities you have. Life is always shifting. Right before your eyes your body, personality, and thoughts change on a daily basis. This holds true for both teenagers and adults.

Navigating the world, for all of us, is perplexing, terrifying, and yet exciting all at the same time. Though it might seem the world can be bleak at times, there will always be things to amaze us and serve as reminders of the wonders there are to explore.

In today's world, pressures exist all around for children and teens. The looming college life, problems at home, and demands at school can leave teens confused as to who they are and how they should act. One minute you're stressing about getting a good grade on a test and the next you're panicked over wearing the right outfit to impress your crush. Getting a good grade can feel as important as who you're going to kiss for the first time.

While trying to fight your way through the jungle of junior high and high school, there are many decisions to make. Sometimes it feels

like you're playing a video game and you have to choose between option A or B, both of which have unpredictable consequences and benefits. Depending on the situation, teachers and parents can turn from a comfort to the source of our anger. Our best friends can be the ones we're envious of the most and any sort of romantic relationship is full of complications.

During this entire time, our minds and bodies are transforming from the children we used to be into the adults we're going to become.

Throughout this book, there are two main important points that will be expanded on:

1. How to be cool
2. How to do this while staying out of trouble

Spreading gossip, lying, and getting involved in other people's business can be hard to resist, especially as a pre-teen trying to traverse this crazy world. The problem many teens struggle with is they simply don't know how to do this.

It feels natural to want to jump in with the gossip because it's easy and everyone else is doing it. It's a way to follow the crowd and know exactly what's next. Or, going against the norms can also give you an exact formula for how to act, dress, and think. However, getting too caught up with labels or the thoughts and opinions of other people can be the very thing that keeps you from success as a teen.

By following these five steps, you can define your voice while also discovering who you are for lifetime success:

1. Build your confidence
2. Manage your emotions
3. Start to know your personality
4. Manage anxiety
5. Show that off

Later in the book, I'll also cover the things that will never be cool under any circumstances. But, the coolest thing you could ever do is allow your true self to show and embrace who this individual is. Only by practicing these steps as both a teen an adult will you be able to flourish.

CHAPTER 1:
Building Confidence

When was the last time you looked at someone and thought, "Wow they're cool?" There is something about them you admire, but you may not be able to put your finger on it. Maybe you even feel a little envious, wondering what it is about them that you don't have.

Fear, nervousness, and anxiety are the biggest roadblocks to being cool. Many of these feelings come from the same insecurities. You might be scared to order a pizza over the phone or make a dentist appointment without a parent's help. Though there are obviously scary things out there, these seemingly small things can also set off an unsettling feeling of anxiety and fear.

It's these internal jittery feelings that not only make us feel awkward but can cause deep, negative emotions that are hard to manage. Being constantly under pressure in a stressful environment can cause anger to build up inside of us, leading to a desire to act out.

There's no easy formula for how to impress others while also striving for success. But, one thing the "cool kids" have in common is that they carry themselves with confidence. Usually, this means that they are not afraid to embrace who they are. No matter what happens, other people will always have their own thoughts and we can't necessarily change them. If you can get to the root of some of your darker feelings, you'll learn to manage those challenging emotions you sometimes experience.

Understand Your Insecurities

Insecurity is anything that causes you to second guess yourself. Any sort of negative trait you attribute to who you are as a person can reflect an insecurity. The things that people make fun of you for or something that you worry about every day might fall into this category. If you don't like the way your face looks, wish you had different hair, or are embarrassed by your clothes, any of these specific things could be considered an insecurity. Sometimes simply feeling stupid or not important enough can also be an insecurity. Having these insecurities is the opposite feeling of having confidence.

What is it that causes this lack of confidence? First, you can look at the people closest to you and how they talk to you and about you. Do you constantly have people around you who are putting you down? Do you have bullies in school, or even family members at home, who tell you that you are dumb, ugly, or not important?

Being surrounded by negative people, people that don't believe in you, can start to rub off on how you judge yourself. You may start to believe what they say about you. Other people might also talk about themselves negatively. Maybe your mom is always talking negatively about her body or her self-worth. This can create the language that we use to speak about ourselves as well. If you grew up in a household where everybody was mean all the time, it can seem normal to use that negative language now.

We also have pressures at school that tell us how we should act, think, and feel. Classmates might pressure you into doing something that you're uncomfortable with. Maybe you feel stress because you want to wear the right clothes to fit in with other people.

Sometimes it's simply the voice in our own head that tells us we are not good enough. What are some of the negative thoughts you have about yourself? Start listening to your self-talk and then you can recognize when you are being your own worst enemy. We can find ourselves saying terrible things to ourselves that are simply not true. By changing some of the language we use in our minds and with our families, we can start to be more confident. Begin to speak more kindly to yourself, just like you would to a good friend.

One thing that we are scared of is failure. Whether you don't want to lose the game in gym class, or you are stressed about getting good grades on a test. It's important to remember that embracing failure can be important. That does not mean you are a failure. It's just that everyone fails when they try new things, the important thing is to look at the failure as a lesson and learn from it. Anyone who accomplished great things, failed many times before they got it right.

Embrace Failure

Failure is embarrassing! Especially if it's in front of your friends. But, it can be a way to learn more about yourself. By making mistakes or failing, you understand what not to do next time you are in the same situation. For example, if you don't study for a test coming up and you fail the test, next time you know how important it is to make sure that you study.

Fearing the outcome of any situation can make you afraid to try in the first place. If you are fearful that you will embarrass yourself in a school play, you might not want to audition even if you have dreams of being an actor or a theater performer one day. However, failure is a natural part of life. The older you get, the more mistakes you make and the more you learn. If you begin to look at mistakes as a way to hone your skills, then slowly, you can begin to lose your fear of them and find the lessons they have to teach you.

Messing up one time doesn't mean you need to feel bad forever. You can look at why it was that you lost that game or got a bad grade on that test and determine the reason for that failure. Michael Jordan didn't make his high school varsity basketball team his sophomore year. Imagine if he never tried again because he failed the first time. Years later, he told people that, whenever he was tired of practicing for varsity tryouts for the next year, he visualized the list hanging on the gym door without his name on it and it motivated him to keep going. Instead of being embarrassed by his failure, he used the lesson as motivation for doing things differently.

By noticing these things, it makes it easier to know how to avoid failure the next time around. Practice is extremely important. Nobody is good at anything they do on the first try. Some people might seem more naturally talented in a specific area, but all experts and professionals had to start somewhere.

The outcome is never quite as scary in the end as it seemed before. For example, imagine that you are afraid to go on a roller coaster. When you look at that roller coaster, the hill is so high, you hear people screaming, and you see how fast it flies by. It's terrifying to imagine being at the top of that hill and looking down. However, your friends force you to go on and you ride it having the time of your life. While it looks scary before, it wasn't nearly as bad as the things that you imagined in your head.

As you navigate through middle school, remember that practice is the way that you will become an expert. While you might embarrass yourself once or twice along the way, it will be worth it in the end when you can show off all of your new skills and talents. No one ever becomes good at something without practice. If you want to really excel at anything, you'll have to fail at it first.

Being Your Own Best Friend

Making friends throughout middle school is part of the fun. When you are older, you may not remember what you learned in class, but you will always remember your best friend in school and the fun you had with them. Having a support system means enjoying school just a little bit more. When you have a friend to partner up with in class or a buddy with you for gym, these challenging things don't seem so bad.

However, one person you want to be friends with more than anybody else is yourself. Sometimes it sounds silly to think about, but we have to be nice to ourselves with the voice that we use in our head. If you can be as kind to yourself as you are to your best friend, you'll always have someone who is looking out for you - yourself! There will be times when there may not be anyone else who believes in you. Practice makes perfect, so start saying kind things to yourself every day. Then, when you hit hard times, you'll know what to say to yourself to get through it.

Shame is when you make somebody feel bad. Often, people are shamed for things that are out of their control. Shame and making somebody feel guilty do not help them want to be better. Instead, it can make people afraid to do anything at all. Be careful if you use shame in your head. Don't call yourself mean names just because you weren't able to succeed with something. If you notice that you're always talking bad to yourself in your own mind, that might end up coming out with how you talk to people around you. While you might be afraid or feeling nervous around others, remember at the end of the day, you should be your own best friend. If you really enjoy the person who you are on the inside, it's so much easier to be confident as you navigate throughout school.

How to Practice Being More Confident

Be more confident by recognizing that the person inside your head is the one who is in charge of how you feel for the day. Confidence is everything from our thoughts to our actions. Many things are out of our control, but one thing we can control is how we think about ourselves. If you are having negative thoughts about yourself, turn that around and tell yourself that you are pretty great! Pick out clothes and other things that make you feel confident. Even if it doesn't quite fit in with what other people like it doesn't matter as long as it makes you feel good about yourself.

Be confident with your voice. Speak up when somebody is making you upset. You don't have to scream and shout at somebody to get your point across. Use kind words like, "Excuse me," or "Can I please say something?" When you're struggling to find your voice, speak loud and clear to keep your voice from shaking and breaking up.

Paying attention to body language is another way to build confidence. Keep your hands out of your pockets and next to your sides. Lift your shoulders up high and then let them slowly fall back behind you. Keep your chin pointed up and your eyes straight ahead. Take a big deep breath in and close your eyes as you let it fall out. Stand up straight and pretend as though you're pressing your back perfectly against a straight wall. By changing your posture alone, this can help boost your confidence to make it easier to stand up for yourself.

Sometimes you might have to say things that aren't popular. There could be moments where you have to speak up for yourself or even somebody that you care about who might be getting bullied. Remember that what you say might not always be the most popular thing, but it can still be the right thing to say. Even if something is challenging to get out in that moment, it doesn't necessarily mean that people are going to judge you forever. As long as you are not saying something offensive and you are doing your part to stand up for what you truly believe is right, then you have every right to speak your mind and use confidence to do so.

CHAPTER 2:
Managing Emotions

If someone says, "Keep your cool," that usually translates to a more stoic or silent presence. It's not that the person in question who is "cool" doesn't have emotions, but instead they are better at managing those feelings. Stress can cause anger, which can sometimes cause emotional outbursts where you may say things you don't mean. Screaming at a friend can be the result of unmanaged emotions. Gossiping or breaking the rules can sometimes help alleviate negative or confusing emotions. But there are better ways to deal with those feelings.

Emotions lead to thoughts which lead to our actions. If you are a pre-teen that always struggles to get good grades, you might feel better sometimes when misbehaving at school. Acting out can be a way to gain back power when we might feel like we don't have control. Stress at home can lead to the desire to act out in a negative way. You might feel like you can't yell at a parent, but that aggression still exists, causing you to take it out on a friend.

By understanding the emotions as you feel them, you'll have more control over what happens next. Our thoughts can occur naturally, but by becoming more aware of the mental journeys that travel through your brain, it's easy to have stronger, positive, and more productive thoughts to work through the most difficult emotions.

Managing emotions does not mean ignoring them. Your feelings and thoughts will always be there. But rather than letting them be the sole driver of what you do next, you can use them to do something more productive. There is always a choice about how to respond to emotions, they don't have to control you. You can't control what happens to you, but you are the one who decides how to respond.

When you start to understand where some of those negative emotions begin, then you can begin controlling them. Sometimes it feels like our friends are the reason we're struggling or maybe you blame a parent or sibling for some of your challenges. No matter where blame is cast, the sole person in charge of how you choose to express those feelings is you. You can feel anger inside and sometimes that's out of your control. But it's within your capacity to decide whether that anger leads you to punch someone or to walk away.

Negative Thoughts

It's easy to fall into the trap of your own thoughts. Negative thought patterns can leave us feeling mad, sad, or lonely. When we are hard on ourselves, it can influence how we end up treating other people. Having negative thoughts might cause you to make harsh judgments about others. Maybe you bully somebody, make fun of them behind their back, or even call them a mean name to their face. Sometimes this only occurs because we are full of negative feelings about our own lives.

Begin to notice things that are more positive or more negative. When you have positive thoughts, it can literally change the way you feel. It's perfectly fine to have negative thoughts. They're very normal and you'll have them, even when you're an adult. The sooner you start to be more aware of these thoughts, the easier it is to have control over them. You don't have to block out the negative thoughts or feel shameful for having them. Instead, try to be aware of how they make you feel.

One example of negative thought patterns includes black and white thinking. This is the idea that everything has to either be:

- Black or white (100% right or 100% wrong)
- All or nothing
- Good or bad

Black and white thinking eliminates the potential for there to be an alternative truth besides just one end of the spectrum. Imagine that a coin is hanging in the air. One person is standing on one side, and another on the other. Somebody in the middle asks, "What is on the coin?" The person on the right, sees the head and the other has tails.

They argue, because they only see their side. They refuse to believe that anybody else can see another picture. However, there is a third truth. The truth is, both people are right. Sometimes it's okay to have thoughts that fall into the center of thinking.

Black and white thinking would also include the idea that just because you had a bad morning, that means you are going to have a bad day. Sometimes we wake up late and have to skip breakfast, or maybe we have a small argument with a sibling before school. This one thing does not mean that the rest of your day has to be ruined.

Black and white thinking might cause us to judge somebody who does one embarrassing thing so we think we can't be friends with them anymore. Everybody makes mistakes and we're all learning in different ways. If you define a person by one singular thing that occurred, you are not seeing "both sides of the coin."

Another type of negative thinking pattern is making assumptions and believing that everything might be about you. If you see a group of girls snickering in the corner, you might assume that they are laughing at you. Maybe instead they're making jokes about their teacher that they all just had a class with. Jumping to conclusions and making assumptions like this can leave us feeling very negative. Just because a friend didn't text you back, you might jump to the conclusion that they don't like you.

These things can leave us feeling very sad if we accept our feelings rather than looking at the whole of the situation. There is an old saying, "feelings are not facts." This means that sometimes we have feelings that just are not true. You may feel stupid when, in fact, you are a pretty good student struggling with a new concept. Those feelings may come from a place of insecurity in yourself or from a difficult situation at home. When you start to feel really negative where everything feels black and dark and you can't see the other side, try to remember that feelings are not facts. They are just feelings. This newfound perspective will give you the ability to manage your emotions better, so they don't make you act out in ways that you'll regret.

Response Versus Reaction

Acting cool means having your attitude in control. If you really want to be able to hang out with a lot of different people and make new friends, it's best to separate your response from your reaction. Our reaction is often out of our control, but it is how you respond to that which matters the most. For example, if somebody comes up to you in school and says, "I think you're really stupid," you probably will react with shock, anger and confusion at first. Where do they get off coming up and telling you that? Why do they have this idea? You might have hurt feelings.

You could respond by telling them they are stupid as well. You could also respond by punching them or kicking them. Any of these might get you into trouble and lead to an even worse situation. Or you could respond by keeping your cool, brushing it off and walking away. Bullies often go out of their way to get a response from other people. They enjoy making others upset because they feel that pain inside them themselves. By walking away, you show that you are the bigger person. You don't care what they think.

You might still have hurt feelings on the inside and you can express those later on. You can talk it out with a friend or a parent or somebody else you're close with. However, by avoiding a response, you are not giving the bully what they are looking for. You can keep yourself out of trouble while also avoiding any more embarrassing fights. It doesn't hurt to have some witty remarks prepared. However, remember silence is always cooler than trying to make somebody else feel bad.

One thing that's never really cool is to get really mad when you lose. Nobody likes playing games with sore losers and it can make it hard for people to want to be on your team if you're acting aggressive towards them. When somebody makes you upset or something doesn't go your way, again, remember to avoid the desire to lash out or even run from these problems. To cope with these emotions in a productive way, ask yourself, How else can I respond to this situation?

You have a feeling inside of you that's telling you something is not right. What words can you use to express that to somebody else without hurting their feelings? One way to do this is to question how it might feel if someone said it to you. Prepare what you want to say to them but don't forget to consider both sides. By reversing perspectives and putting yourself into the other person's shoes, you ensure that your response is cool, calm, and collected.

Reminders for Emotional Control

Going through middle school can be a very emotional time. There are a few things that can ensure you'll have the coolest attitude as you progress through these tough times.

First and foremost, avoid gossiping at all costs. Though it might seem cool to participate in this witty banter and add funny comments or do impressions of others, it can really come back to bite you in the end. You never know who you can truly trust. Maybe they're going to tell somebody else once they walk away from you. Maybe somebody you didn't realize is sitting around the corner, they were listening to you, and they might end up sharing what you said with that other person.

Gossip can get back to the individual that is being gossiped about and at that point, what was said can be twisted into something much uglier than the words that you initially used. Once people know you gossip, they won't trust you not to gossip about them. If you truly want to make friends, be popular, and have fun experiences with others, find a way to avoid gossip. If you're constantly gossiping to one friend about another, they might start to question if you are doing the same behind their backs.

You don't want to make people afraid to trust you. Making new friends and going through these experiences is something that you'll never get to go through again as a middle schooler. Don't waste your time talking about other people! Everybody has their problems, and we all do weird things from time to time. Making fun of somebody else is never going to make you feel better about yourself. In fact, it'll probably result in you judging yourself way harsher later on.

No matter what happens, as you were struggling with your emotional control, remember to never lie. Just like gossiping, lying will always come back at you and sometimes twice as bad. Lying always leads to bigger problems. Let's face it, it's way easier to just tell the truth! It's tough to keep track of lies and make sure no one figures them out. If you tell the truth all the time, you don't have to keep track of what you said to who.

There are some activities you can do to better control your emotions. For example, try to set aside a little bit of alone time each day to think about things. It's great if you can do this first thing in the morning to prepare for things, but that's not always possible. One way to get that alone time is to go for a short walk each day. Let's call it a mindfulness walk.

If you're feeling upset, stressed, or angry, take a walk around your home, your backyard or even down the driveway and center yourself. If your parents let you, take a quick walk down the street and take a moment to notice something really nice. You might see something in nature that helps calm you down, or you can simply take deep breaths, count your steps and let the negative feelings slowly fade away.

Another act of mindfulness is to simply pick out one color of an item. For example, look for something that's red. Then look around the room and identify all the things that jump out to you which are red. If you are still upset, look for another color. It's a way to break the thoughts in your head and get you in a different place. Sometimes thinking all of these terrible things can start a chain reaction that gets harder to stop the more it goes on. By using mindfulness you're forcing yourself to take a step back; take a deep breath in, and break that downward spiral.

CHAPTER 3:
Get To Know Who You Are

If you ask anyone how to be cool, they will always say, "Just be yourself." It seems simple, but what does that mean? How can you be yourself if you have no concept of who that person is?

It takes a while to know who you are. But, that is part of the fun! It really comes with experiencing new things and discovering what you enjoy the most. As long as you are open to learning more and more about what interests you, you'll be learning who you are at the same time. And, of course, who we are changes over time as well. We are not set in stone, change and growth should be a constant in your life.

Questioning who you are will always be important whether you're 18 or 38. The good thing is, this kind of thought process is the quickest way to internal growth! It leaves you open to finding your path forward, with a future career, or hobby, and it helps you to define the characteristics and beliefs that are important to you as a unique individual.

Trying to copy other people and simply mimic the things that you see may be the quickest way to blend into the crowd. But, you are only putting off the inevitable search for your true passion. We are all unique in our talents and interests and the only way to figure out who you are is to embrace that special uniqueness.

There will always be challenges and experiences that leave you questioning who you are and that's a really good thing. It's during these times that we tend to do the most growing up. It is another opportunity to learn how to handle situations that will come around again and again during life. At the end of the day, no one knows you better than you know yourself.

Values and Beliefs

In order to stand up for something, you have to know what you believe in! What does it mean to have a belief? This can have various meanings, such as:

1. Your religious beliefs
2. Political beliefs
3. Moral beliefs

There are many more, we can learn more about our personal beliefs as we start to talk about things that are important to us. One thing is for certain, as a middle school student, your values and beliefs are going to change as you discover more and more about life and continue to question yourself and everything around you.

Why does it matter to talk about them, then? For starters, you're entering a time when you begin to see the world as it really is, complicated! You're not exactly a kid anymore and your parents will stop trying to shield you from every bad thing that happens. You are growing up and that means they are going to trust you with some hard truths. There are so many problems in the world and it's important to start figuring out how you feel about them. It doesn't mean you can solve all the problems that you encounter, but your beliefs will help you figure out how to approach them.

You'll also start to learn more about our history and all the darker times of the past. Now is a time when the groundwork for your values and beliefs starts to become more prominent than ever. How does this have anything to do with being cool?

Someone who is cool isn't afraid to speak their mind and say how they feel. A person who is always changing their mind or just agreeing with everyone else doesn't stand out. Those who are admired by others dare to be different from the rest and will sharpen their voice. Sometimes this means going in the opposite direction of others, but it can still be really powerful to be fearless with your voice.

If you were taught a certain religion growing up and you are proud of that, don't be afraid to voice those opinions. You might have doubts and that's fine! It could lead you to a path better suited for your future or it could strengthen your beliefs and values even further. The same goes for any political views. You're still young enough to not have to make any decisions, but it's never too late to stay informed.

What's most important above all else is to remember these beliefs and values are your own. Not only does sticking to the same thing everyone else believes keep you blended into the crowd, but it can leave you feeling sad inside if you're not being true to who you are.

Likes and Interests

Just like you should hone your beliefs and values as you learn more, your likes and interests are also important to develop. These, too, can be different from your parents, friends, and anyone else you know! It's common for parents to encourage their teens into the same things they liked, such as sports or activities like dancing. While you might find these things interesting, remember that isn't always the case. It's OK to develop your own personal opinions, thoughts and hobbies. The point is it needs to be interesting to you!

Those who are really good at what they do usually genuinely enjoy doing it. If you hate volleyball but play it to make your mom happy, you might end up dreading everyday after school because of practice. They will probably understand, especially if there is a different sport or activity you are interested in. Most of the time, parents love to see their kids make choices for themselves, but if not, look for ways to compromise. It's an opportunity to share your voice without anger, have that discussion!

In order to continue to grow your skills and develop new strengths, pick out things that are interesting but also challenging. To start, pick a hobby that's not related to school. This might be painting, knitting, a sport, making movies, photography, volunteering at a pet clinic, baking, gardening, collecting, and so on. Whatever you do, find a hobby that you can call your own without the pressure of performance and school looming over you. This hobby can be an escape when you're stressed and also serve to impress people. (Playing a musical instrument is always a great asset!)

In addition to this, make sure you participate in at least one activity at school. Whether it's a club or a sport, it's a good way to find people who enjoy doing the same things as you. Not only do you make friends in the process, but you also get to grow your skills for something that can be valuable on a college application in the future!

Always explore new areas of interest. Ignore just what others strictly like and seek out different avenues of the things you specifically enjoy. Of course, if you like popular hobbies that's fine as well!

Stick to things for a certain period of time to make sure you've given it a fair chance, but remember being young means you'll have a lot of opportunities to try new things and figure out what you truly like. Though you might have invested a few months into a hobby, that doesn't mean you have to invest three years of your life down the road! Know when to keep persevering, but remember that walking away can simply mean turning in a different direction that can also lead to success.

Growth Mindset

Having a growth mindset will be one of the "coolest" things you can do as a middle schooler, high schooler, and adult. When people don't like to try new things, have a fixed mindset. Those who resist anything different and aren't willing for new changes can often find themselves stuck in this type of thinking and it can prevent new opportunities. If you always had the same ice cream flavor, you'd never get to discover new kinds you like!

To have a growth mindset, eliminate the words "can't" or "won't" from your thoughts. Don't say, "I won't try out new sports. What's the point? I can't do it anyway." Instead, say, "I'm willing to try out a new activity. Even if I'm not great at it at least I know now instead of wondering about it forever!" A fixed mindset means getting stuck on one thing rather than exploring all of the many options that are truly out there in the world.

Remember to have patience for things to change. Sometimes what you want to happen will take a few days, weeks, or even months. If you want to be a faster runner, it doesn't occur just overnight. Those who are resistant to change and are impatient in the process will always end up stuck in the same place. Not many people are happy when they don't give themselves the freedom to explore!

Challenge your thoughts as you have them. Don't think all your thoughts are bad, but as one comes into your mind consider:

1. Where that thought came from
2. What it means
3. How it makes you feel

Is this a belief that was instilled in you by someone else, like a parent or sibling? Did you hear it on a TV show? What is the validity - or truth - of the statement? Was it made by an expert or just a loud person with an opinion? What does this thought mean to you? Is it simply a reflection of something you heard? Is it a new thought that you just made up? How does it make you feel? Is it encouraging you or scaring you? Never fear trying new things because this is the way you might discover the next thing you love!

CHAPTER 4:
Handling Stress

An overabundance of stress can negatively affect our emotional state. As a teen, you don't have to worry about experiencing a shortage of stress. Though it can feel overwhelming, there are ways to manage stress.

Take things slow. It might seem like everyone around you has a boyfriend/girlfriend, is partying or drinking, and doing other things that put pressure on you. This is not true at all. It's easy to make assumptions based on what you see or hear around you. However, don't feel pressured into these things because even if that were the case, that doesn't mean you have to do the same.

Dealing with one stressful thing is hard, but the more there are, the more pressure there is on you. At a certain point it's hard to function, making your focus fuzzy and your thoughts scrambled. The more overwhelmed you feel the harder it is to manage tasks, whether you have five or fifty. The issue isn't always how much stuff you have to do but rather the approach to completing these tasks.

Take breaks when you can. Life is short and time seems like it's zooming by as a teenager. But that doesn't mean you can't still take breaks. You might have to apply for scholarships, sign up for classes, get a date to prom, and do everything else in between, but you still can have fun and enjoy your time. There's no rush to be an adult. Maintain responsibilities as needed but when the opportunity presents itself, don't be afraid to take the plunge.

Remove yourself from stressful situations that overwhelm you at the end of the day. If you truly cannot manage stress after everything else you've tried, maybe it's time to make a harder decision. It could mean stepping away from an activity or saying "No" to a friend. Remember it's OK to give yourself breathing room so you come back even stronger to knock out the next task.

Procrastination

Procrastination is the habit of pushing things off and never getting them done on time. Adults and teens alike suffer from this bad habit. People often procrastinate doing things like homework and chores. You've probably procrastinated before without even knowing what it meant. Imagine your mom asked you to clean up before she got home from work. Even though you had plenty of time, you still waited until the last ten minutes before she got home.

Procrastination can make us take too long to get things done and causes unnecessary stress. A project you can easily do in ten minutes might take all night because you're sitting there scrolling through the internet instead of trying to finish the project. It can make us feel rushed like we don't have enough time to get the project done, but in reality, we just haven't managed our time well. It takes time and practice to get good at organizing your time!

Procrastination is a way to push a pain off. Sometimes homework isn't fun and you simply don't feel like doing it right now. However, by not doing it you're only prolonging your misery, making it harder to finish up at the end of the day. By pushing something off, you get to avoid thinking about it. However, your brain never truly forgets, meaning you don't even get to enjoy what you're doing.

Sometimes, procrastination occurs because we are fearing that we'll fail at the end. If you are working on a project in a difficult subject and you don't trust that you're going to do well, of course you'll try to avoid completing that task. Finishing it may mean you're one step closer to failure, so it's that much harder to want to give your effort to that task.

To avoid procrastinating in that case, ask for help if you need it. Whether it's from a teacher, classmate, or your parents, the help of others can either give you the motivation needed to keep going or they could give you a morsel of information needed to finish up the project in the best way possible.

If you're simply bored with the project, look for a fun way to do it. Can you do your homework in the backyard instead of at your desk? Getting outside and setting up a little campsite in a fun spot can be a way to bring a little more excitement to an otherwise boring task. Can you and your friends use the format of a game you like to quiz each other, or better yet, can you come up with your own game? Get creative with how to avoid procrastination and you might find it becomes a habit you keep for a lifetime.

One final tip for avoiding procrastination is to remember to limit your screen time. It's really easy to get REALLY distracted. So, when you have something to do, put the phone down, and get to work. Building this type of discipline will help you throughout your life. But, that's easier said than done...

Managing Screen Time

If you have access to a phone, tablet, computer, or gaming system, you might find that you are reaching for it without even realizing it. These devices are the best! You can talk to friends, play games, read interesting things, share information, and do so much more. Unfortunately, not only do they take time away from us but we could even get in trouble with them. You might spend too much time and break household rules or maybe you find yourself the victim of cyberbullying.

To keep your cool at school while still succeeding, remember that more screen time doesn't necessarily mean more popularity. Too much screen time can make us lose focus. Why read a book for school when you can spend that time playing video games? Unfortunately, this also means wasting time away that could be put towards learning something more important.

Getting online, especially social media, might mean seeing things that make you upset or feel bad. For example, there's tons of photo editing used on famous celebrities' pictures, so their perfect bodies can put pressures on young girls to wish they had the same. Even looking at peers' pictures might make you feel left behind and as if you're missing out on something great. In reality, people only show what they want others to see, and that means you're missing the reality of their stresses and worries that we all experience in some forms.

Make sure that if your parents aren't limiting screen time, set some limits for yourself. This is to simply make it easier to focus and to ensure you don't lower your confidence to the point that you "lose your cool."

One way to do this, is to avoid sleeping with your phone on. We require a deep, undisturbed sleep, so buzzing notifications all night can keep you from achieving that. Another option is to wait a bit in the morning before reaching for the phone, give yourself time to think about your day first and get yourself organized. Set aside specific times of the day to get your social media done and then try not to check it constantly. How many times a day do you want to do social media? Set that up and stick to it.

Stress-Relieving Techniques

You're never too young to know how to manage stress. It's a chemical response in the body. If you're presented with something scary, stress signals tell you to react. Stress responses are important in all animals. If a cat is scared it will hiss and scratch to defend itself. If you were to walk down a trail and come face to face with a snake, your stress response would tell you to either run away or fight the snake. In that case, the stress response is a good thing! But when we are getting that reaction over things that are not life-threatening, it can start to wear down our health.

This response was helpful in caveman times when a saber-toothed tiger might jump out and attack us at any minute. Then our heart rate increases and pumps the blood away from our digestive tract and to our muscles so we can run. Hormones, like adrenaline, flood our bodies and make us hyper-reactive to any small stimulation. Sugar from our storage in our liver and muscles pours out in case we need that energy for running.

If our bodies experience the stress response all day long, we can end up with high blood sugar, poor digestion, trouble sleeping and anxiety, it even makes it difficult to lose weight. All because our physical system is still set up to expect the tiger to jump out at us at any moment.

If you aren't aware of this, it could mean being stressed out all day long. Perhaps you're always struggling to know what to do next because of intense fear. Not only does it make our minds swirl around until we're dizzy, but it can also leave our bodies feeling achy and tired.

To manage stress, remember that there are four key elements to consider:

1. Diet
2. Sleep schedule
3. Exercise routine
4. Stress levels

As a middle schooler you likely don't have a ton of money to manage your eating schedule, but when the choices are presented choose wisely. Pick naturally colorful foods like fruits and vegetables. Portion size is important. Exercise is something you can control. If you're not getting any at school, try to participate more in at home activities.

Pets can be great stress relievers. Spend more time playing with and petting your home's cats and dogs. If you don't have any, why not ask a parent or guardian to volunteer at an animal shelter?

Find an activity to make you feel good about yourself. Pick one creative thing to do to express how you are feeling. Whether you want to write songs or simply use a pen and notebook to sketch, seek new ways to create something new. You can show how you are feeling and what those emotions might look like through your creative voice.

If you are ever feeling truly overwhelmed and it feels like there is nothing to do to free yourself from stress, reach out to a parent or a school counselor. They can give you the resources needed to feel better rather than having to take drastic measures to do that yourself.

CHAPTER 5:
Looking Cool

While it might seem like you need the most expensive name brand clothes and the best body and hair to be cool, that's not the case! Being cool is a feeling inside of you. It's not a uniform or script to memorize. However, when we combine our appearance with what we feel inside, that can make us have an even stronger sense of who we are. If you're a free spirit, wearing a suit everyday can make you feel out of whack. If you like to be having comfortable clothes on, then dressy or loud clothes might make you feel out of place. Matching what you feel inside with what you feel outside will create a harmonious balance, and vice versa.

Having a unique style is cooler than matching any exact image of what someone else has presented to you. Showing who you truly are through the things you choose to wear shows to other people that you are not afraid to express your voice. Those who are noticed the most are the ones who aren't afraid to be a little different. Sometimes you might find a look that doesn't quite work but needs some accessories, becoming who we are requires a little trial and error, but have fun with it!

Who you are will show through no matter what you wear, and that's the most important thing to remember. A truly confident person that believes they are beautiful will look good in a garbage bag. Hopefully you have better clothes than that, but don't forget that looking good is more than just the materials you decide to drape around your body.

Good Hygiene

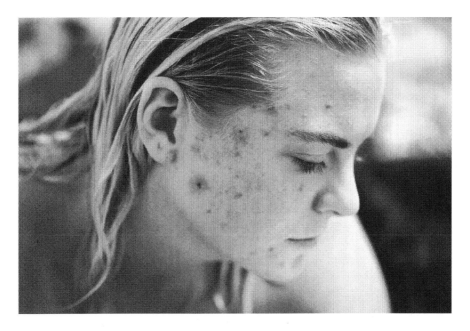

No matter what you wear, good hygiene is important. At a time when your body is rapidly changing, taking special care to keep everything in line is important. To have good hygiene, remember five important elements:

1. Teeth
2. Body odor
3. Hair
4. Skin
5. Nails

Having good hygiene is not feminine, despite what stereotypes might have you believe. Throughout history makeup is often associated with women and feminine things, for example, but makeup is not hygiene. Having good hygiene means that you are clean, it's as simple as that. Having good hygiene is important for your own body by eliminating excess bacteria and sweat that could cause infections and heavy odors.

Start by making sure to brush your teeth twice every single day. Right when you wake up in the morning is a good time to start because you brush all the bacteria off that had been collecting in your mouth overnight. You can also wait until after breakfast if you'd prefer to brush the food off as well. Then, brush your teeth before going to bed to prevent bacteria from developing on your teeth all night.

Your body odor occurs because of the way your body breaks down the bacteria that is present in sweat. The more you sweat, the more body odor likely to be present. Body odor occurs wherever there are crevices and more closed-off spots on your body, most commonly your armpits. Use deodorant before going anywhere and remember that perfume and cologne won't mask the smell and will instead simply combine with body odor. Wash your body once a day on average. If you skip a weekend day, it's normal, but since you're going to school everyday, showering is important. Exfoliate your skin to help create a smoother appearance and promote healthy skin growth.

Hair doesn't need to be washed daily. Hair should be washed two or three times a week. Everyone's hair is different. If yours is more oily, three or even four times a week might be necessary. Those with dry hair should stick to twice a week or even just once a week. Grooming your hair shows you not only are clean, but you also care about yourself, and that boosts confidence.

Your skin will be another area to focus on, especially as a teen. Acne might start to pop up, so paying attention to what you eat is essential. Externally, remember to use a separate wash for your face for specific acne treatments for optimal results. Use a lotion as well for a smoother appearance.

Don't pop pimples! No matter how much you might have the urge, let them naturally fade and use a spot treatment. Trying to pop them almost always makes them bigger and more painful. Oily skin might require more frequent washes. Remember this isn't just to make you look good on the outside but to feel your best so you're not afraid to be yourself! A healthy diet, free of junk food and sodas, can often help your skin look better.

Hydration is essential for good skin. Always drink water and have a bottle you can carry around (if your school permits). Hydration is essential through beverages other than soda or juice. It helps flush out the body and provides important hydrogen atoms where needed in your body.

Finally, remember to groom your nails. Again, nail grooming might seem like a more feminine thing. But men's fingernails should be just as groomed as well. Trim your nails as needed. Don't let them get too long or else dirt will get trapped underneath. If you do decide to grow them long for aesthetic reasons, make sure to clean out underneath them at least once a day. Even though they might appear clean, so much more gets trapped under your nails than you'd think. Then whatever you do with your hands gets exposed to those germs.

What to Wear

While brand name clothes might seem cool, it's not the only way to dress the part. Big expensive brands want you to believe that this is the truth, so you spend all your money on their product. A white t-shirt is a white t-shirt whether it has a red box logo on the front or not. Don't feel the pressure to label yourself with the labels of an expensive company.

Pick out clothes that help express what you're feeling on the inside.

If you are calm and quiet by nature, pick basic staples in softer colors. If you're wild and vibrant, don't be afraid to show that as well. Your personality doesn't even have to match your clothes! You might be the craziest, wackiest, funniest person ever but still decide to wear blue jeans and a white tee everyday. That's all entirely up to you.

If you don't have access to expensive clothing, remember to use thrift stores when you can. You can find completely unique and vintage pieces that no one else has, and you'd be surprised how often you'll find popular labels there. How can you dress up a simple t-shirt? How can you dress down a nicer dress? Consider these different things and play around with your style. See if you can go through a relative or a friend's closet to either take what they don't want or simply swap clothes that both of you would rather give away.

As far as makeup goes, wear what you enjoy wearing. Start with one thing at a time. Usually mascara or lipstick might be the first place to start. Slowly add things in. Practice at home and watch tutorials on YouTube to get tips on what and what not to do. Don't share makeup with others, especially anything that goes directly on the skin (like mascara) or carries more germs (like lipstick).

CHAPTER 6:

Things That Will Never Be "Cool"

What is and isn't cool will always be subjective. In other words, it's all about your opinion. Some people think being the captain of the football team is the coolest thing ever, while others would rather admire the lead guitarist in a band. You might even think both are pretty cool! However, there are a few things that are never cool, no matter what the circumstances.

These next three sections cover areas that you should never participate in but can sometimes be hard to avoid. If you're in a group with five friends and they all start to bully someone, standing up against that could mean ending a friendship or getting some of that bullying yourself. But, there will be people that are going to respect your strength. They may be afraid to show it right away, but you will be setting a great example for them.

It might be hard, and it might mean you lose a few friends, or the admiration from people you label as "cool." But if they participate in that kind of behavior, should you really be that concerned about their opinion of you? Why would you want to base your self-worth on the ideas and opinions of those who think bullying or any form of violence is "cool?"

Bullying

Sometimes bullying is easy to see. A group of students pushing one around or calling them names is a clear-cut case. However, more subtle forms of bullying exist in places you might not always look. Types of bullying include:

1. Physical (punching, pushing, poking, etc.)
2. Verbal (name calling, belittling, berating, laughing at, etc.)
3. Cyberbullying (direct hate through messages/comments, posts mocking others, etc.)
4. Exclusion (intentionally not inviting someone, not allowing someone in an open club or group, etc.)

If you notice any of these types of bullying, or are the victim yourself, the first thing to do is remove the victim from the bullies. Don't think about retaliation. Get yourself or the other person to a safe spot as quickly as possible. If you don't think you can do this on your own, seek help immediately. If there is a group of four students beating up one, you likely should not insert yourself as you will both get hurt. Your efforts are better served finding help ASAP.

Next, ask if they are OK. They might have injuries that you can't see, or maybe they simply want to talk it out. Finally, seek out those in charge for proper punishment, discipline, or reprimanding of the actual bullies. Even if it's your own group of friends who are hurting someone, trying to take matters into your own hands can be too much to handle at once. Bullying is never OK.

What might seem like harmless teasing to you could be someone else's final straw.

Pressuring Others

Peer pressure is real and shows up in the most random places. Be wary if someone tries to pressure you into:

1. Drinking alcohol
2. Doing drugs
3. Having sex
4. Committing a crime
5. Doing anything that makes you uncomfortable

While we are all in control of our actions, trying to persuade others to do bad things is never going to help anyone. If you notice someone getting pressured, follow the same steps as you would for someone who's being bullied. No matter what someone says to you, they cannot pressure you to do anything you don't want to do.

Avoiding Education

School is cool! Of course, not all of it seems that way, however. It is true you will have some boring teachers and some subjects cause you to question, "What's the point of learning this?" Despite bad experiences with education you have, learning itself is incredibly valuable.

Knowledge will always be more valuable than grades. While acing the test and getting high marks is admirable, don't make that your sole focus. When we do this, what ends up happening is the information is mesmerized quickly the night before and then easily forgotten once the test has been taken. If you approach your subjects with a greater willingness to learn rather than just memorize, it will be easier to take the test and also apply that information in other areas.

No matter how dumb, boring, or silly a topic seems, never underestimate your education or let another person make you feel bad or silly for wanting to expand your knowledge. Your mind will always be your greatest tool so you may as well use it!

CONCLUSION

The key to being a cool teenager isn't trying to fit into a mold or impress others. The point should be to find out a little more about who you are and embrace that person. Don't be afraid to be who you want to be, seek out things you like, and always question the world around you.

The older you get the easier it is to define our beliefs and values. Though intelligence doesn't equate with age, there are some things that can only be learned with experience. Embrace this idea and be mindful of what you'll be learning along the way. Keep track of your thoughts to notice the different type of person you're growing into.

There is no need to put pressure on yourself to know exactly who you are right now. You're at the beginning of an incredible journey and the idea that this will be ever-changing should be embraced.

Remember to work on building confidence. This will get you that job. Confidence will lead you to a new group of friends. It will help you find someone you love. It will simply make it easier to get up in the morning. When you are lacking confidence, dive deep to the root of those insecurities. What would you tell your best friend to overcome these doubts?

Keep emotions under control. A lack of understanding and power over your feelings can lead to a greater disadvantage than advantage in the long run. Even if you don't know why you are feeling a certain way, try to refrain from acting out in a way that will have negative consequences for longer than just this moment. It's easy to act on impulse but always remove yourself from the situation if you have to.

Recognize your personality when you see it and don't feel the need to hide that away. We make discoveries about ourselves and sometimes those are good and sometimes it's downright scary. What if we find out we don't want to be the person our parents expect us to be? At the end of the day, you have to put your happiness first if you ever want true success. Milestones and accomplishments won't take you everywhere you need to go. Feeling good about yourself and proud of the things you've done will be more valuable than anything else.

Manage stress before it takes over your mind. Stress is natural and normal, and we will never be able to completely free ourselves from it. However, we will be able to better manage those feelings so our day to day lives aren't so uncomfortable. Find activities you enjoy and stick to them to feel better on a consistent basis.

Create an appearance you're happy and comfortable with and don't let anyone else force this identity onto you. While a lot of this journey is about finding and nurturing yourself, remember to consider others along the way.

Becoming a Better Student, Friend, and "Child"

Maintaining healthy relationships is important and teaches you more about who you are while providing a wonderful support you can rely on. Life is fun on its own but it's a lot more exciting when we get to share our thoughts and ideas with other people.

Remember your teachers. They work hard to make sure that you get a good education. Sometimes they're wrong and they might even come off rude but remember you're not the only student they have. They are learning just as much in this process as you are!

Our friends can become lifelong companions. In a world with so much technology it's easy to stay connected to friends, so don't think of any relationship as disposable. A true friendship involves wanting to hear what the other person has to think and sharing different ideas and opinions. Though sometimes you might hit some rough patches, working through those can create a stronger bond in the end.

Finally, remember your parents, and those who you consider parents. They may not always be blood; a lot of us aren't lucky enough to have great parents. But, if we look around, there is probably an adult who cares about us deeply. Maybe it's a teacher, or a school janitor. Maybe it's your principal, or the parents of a friend. Whoever it is, make sure they know you appreciate them. If you are lucky enough to have parents who really care about you, even if they make mistakes sometimes, make sure they know you love them, too.

The road ahead is a bumpy one, but with good friends and loved ones along the way, the easier it will be when you hit those rough patches. At the end of the day you're going to be your best support, so remember to look out for yourself and always make decisions with your health in mind.

REFERENCES

Ditch the Label. (n.d.). 7 Things You Can Do If You Witness Someone Being Bullied. Retrieved from https://www.ditchthelabel.org/witness-someone-being-bullied

Elias, M. (2017). Helping Your Students Identify Their Values. Retrieved from https://www.edutopia.org/blog/helping-your-students-identify-their-values-maurice-elias

Felman, A. (2017). What's to Know About Body Odor? Retrieved from https://www.medicalnewstoday.com/articles/173478

Gallo, A. (2011). How to Build Confidence. Retrieved from https://hbr.org/2011/04/how-to-build-confidence

Grohol, J. (2019). 15 Common Cognitive Distortions. Retrieved from https://psychcentral.com/lib/15-common-cognitive-distortions

Popova, M. (Fixed vs. Growth: The Two Basic Mindsets That Shape Our Lives. Retrieved from https://www.brainpickings.org/2014/01/29/carol-dweck-mindset

Psychology Today. (n.d.). Stress. Retrieved from https://www.psychologytoday.com/us/basics/stress

Scholastic Parents Staff. (n.d.). 13 Tips for Success From a Middle School Principal. Retrieved from https://www.scholastic.com/parents/school-success/school-involvement/13-tips-success-middle-school-principal.html

Sewickley Academy. (n.d.). Sewickley Academy: Resource Blog for Parents. Retrieved from https://blog.sewickley.org/things-i-wish-i-knew-in-middle-school-by-logan-16

Wild, M. (2010). 7 Steps to Succeeding in Middle School. Retrieved from https://www.greatschools.org/gk/articles/succeeding-in-middle-school

Printed in Great Britain
by Amazon